I0475427

A PEEK BEHIND THE SIGNS

Juhree Fletcher

Copyright © 2011 Juhree Fletcher
All rights reserved.
ISBN: 1451590997
ISBN 13: 9781451590999

A PEEK BEHIND THE SIGNS

INTRODUCTION

Wish this was a get-rich-quick guide, but it is not. It is simply a collection of tips on how to maximize property value and survive the sale process with a sense of humor. Lessons I have learned from over twenty years of helping clients, and from remodeling more than ten properties. Think of it as things your Realtor© would tell you if they weren't so polite. If I insult your decorating choices with my advice, which I probably will, then I apologize.

I also apologize to agents who do not share my views. It is my goal to help sellers understand the hurdles we face. This is especially important these days, when homes stay on the market for so long and we are there so often it would be easier if we just moved in.

To all homeowners, I share your pain. Whether your home is a six-hundred-square-foot mobile home or a twelve-thousand-square-foot estate, we are all suffering. Please accept my stories in the context in which they are intended, to help you through my experiences.

SO YOU REALLY WANT TO SELL NOW?

I sell real estate in Los Angeles and the market is pretty gloomy for sellers. If the same is true where you live, you must have thought long and hard about listing. At least you own something of value. Have hope, homes are selling every day.

The following ideas can make the sales process more profitable and less stressful. The first point, and the most important one, is to think of your sale as a business venture. You are not selling a basket of good times and memories. You are selling an investment. Keep emotions out of your decisions.

It is a horrible time to sell, but a great time to buy. If you are selling in order to move up to a larger home or better neighborhood, then smart move. Real estate sages say the money is made on buying well, not in selling.

If you may need to sell within the next couple of years, now is probably the optimum time. Values can fall further and interest rates can rise. Postponing would hurt. On the other hand, real estate has historically proven to be a profitable long-term investment. If you are facing a loss and do not need to sell, it may be smarter to ride out the storm. Economists vary in their predictions on how long this could take.

My first purchase was a tiny, I mean tiny, bungalow in the San Fernando Valley that cost thirty-six thousand dollars. This was over twenty-five years ago at the "height of the market." Everyone told us we were crazy, but we needed the write-off and bought anyway. One year later we sold the house for sixty-seven thousand dollars, again, at the "height of the market." This house is worth over eight hundred thousand dollars today. At that time in my life I never dreamt that real estate would become such an important asset. If you can afford what you buy, over time, it will be good to you.

Properties that have major drawbacks suffer most in a buyer's market. With high inventory and many choices, buyers are not likely to choose homes that are hanging over a freeway or are in the flight path of an airport. These sellers should at least choose the most active selling season in their area and price aggressively.

Love your home, but it is too small? Many contractors are looking for work. Adding on could be a good alternative. This will also add value to the property. Another option may be to convert your existing home into a rental. Talk to a financial expert to see if you and your property qualify.

Whatever your path, please be committed to selling before you list. At the very least, be honest. If you are testing the market before deciding, please share this with your Realtor©. Many agents will be happy to market your property in order to use it as bait to attract clients. It can be frustrating, expensive, and disheartening for an agent to work hard for someone who decides not to sell at the last minute.

One of my clients was a tough Southern cookie who had lived in her home for over fifty years. She proudly declared to me and her daughters that she was ready to move to the beach. I was new in the business and glad to have the listing, but I could not get her to lower the price. For years her gracious-yet-run-down Spanish duplex was priced way over market. I tried nicely to resign the listing, but each time it expired, she convinced me she was ready to sell. By stalling, she was able to put off the move and enjoy all the attention that selling generated. Finally we got an offer that she accepted.

Going through the offer item by item, sipping coffee, all went well until we reached the length of escrow. I asked how long she needed to pack and be ready to move. Her eyes got wide, her mouth gaped open, and she slid to the floor in a faint. The reality of actually moving was overwhelming. As soon as the paramedics left, I took the sign down. We remained friends, but she never moved.

Make sure you are prepared to move before you put up the sign.

"I understand you think your home is worth three million. Unfortunately, comps in the neighborhood put it closer to one and a half."

PICK A NUMBER, ANY NUMBER

Nothing turns a lovely visit with prospective sellers to a chilly standoff faster than introducing sales comparables and a market analysis. Instead of devouring these statistics as the mathematic answer to the value of their property, many proud homeowners get lost in the arguments of why their home is worth more than their neighbors. Please don't do this. Be objective. Neither you nor your Realtor© can determine the exact market value of your home.

Sales are mainly a result of supply and demand. The buyers will tell you what your home is worth. Then their lender will weigh in. Sorry, but your opinion doesn't really matter. If you are resolute on getting a specific price for your property, then you may not sell. Be prepared to accept the highest price offered, whatever that may be. The more competitively you price your home, the sooner it will sell. Price your home too high, it will sit there, costing you time, carrying costs, and in a falling market, value.

Every seller should take the time to look at homes in their neighborhood that are on the market. The better educated, the better decisions you will make. At the very least, drive by your competition. Look at interiors online. Note the size, cost per square foot, length of time on the market, general condition, and age of kitchen and baths. Especially compare homes with the same bedroom and bathroom count as yours. Picture your home from a buyer's point of view. What price would attract you? Be realistic, and be ready to reduce if you are not getting action.

Realtors© will give you data on recent sales, and it is easy to acquire information on active listings. The online value services can be helpful with sale prices if all the houses in your neighborhood are similar, without too many variables. Otherwise, best to rely on agents who have sold a large variety of homes. Get a market analysis from at least two or three agents and ask them to be conservative. If the market is changing, expect your projection to change.

Interview several Realtors© before hiring. Personal referrals are the best way to find a good one, but another option is to talk to the agents who have listings in your neighborhood. They will have firsthand knowledge of the activity and competition. Choose someone who is a member of the National Association of Realtors© to ensure premium quality of service. Select an agent who does this full-time, so they are readily available. Agents who have bought and sold their own homes will personally relate to your concerns. Go for quality of the person, not status of their company. Torn between two? Hire them both. Chances are they would be glad to work together and share the commission. If they work for separate companies, you will get double exposure.

Speaking of commission, everything is negotiable. However it is not wise to offer reduced commission to the agents representing the buyers, or your house will be at a disadvantage. You do not want agents steering their clients away from your home and towards those who will earn them a larger fee. Agree on a commission that is typical for your area and price range.

Best friends and relatives sometimes make great agents, sometimes they do not. On the plus side, they will have your best interest at heart. On the other hand, they will learn the details of your personal finances, as well as where you hide your dirty laundry. In addition, negotiations can get heated. I have seen beautiful friendships blow up over a few thousand dollars. If you feel pressure to hire a relative or good friend yet are a little skeptical, consider splitting the listing and put a seasoned pro on your team. This may protect your asset and preserve a friendship.

The many homeowners who are upside down in their loan should not be afraid to discuss finances with their agents. We run statistics to verify ownership and encumbrances before a listing is submitted anyway. Your agent can help you devise a strategy and open negotiations with the bank. Do not let the stress take a toll on your health or relationships. It is business. These situations are not uncommon. You are not alone, and things will get better. If facing a short sale or having difficulty paying your mortgage, I encourage you to clean well, eliminate clutter, and list today. Do not worry about spending money on improvements.

During the late eighties, one of my clients had to negotiate a short sale with his lender. We tried to sell for full loan value, but after many months he had to accept a loss. Years later this man was able to buy property again, and now lives securely with profits made by selling a shack on the Pacific Ocean bought for $1.2 million and sold for $3.5 million. Situations can change for you as well.

Remember, Realtors© are your allies. We want the same thing you do, to sell your home for top dollar as quickly as possible!

*"Wow, I don't believe I have ever seen so many
snow globes in one room before!"*

LIGHTS, CANDLES, ACTION!

When we open our doors at the end of a long day, we are met with comfortable, familiar surroundings. The question is, what do strangers see?

Imagine entering a suite at a five-star hotel. Guests are met with soothing, orderly, fragrant luxury. Of course these hotels spend millions of dollars with advice from top designers. You do not need to spend millions, but a few of their practices can make your home more inviting.

Begin by getting organized. The absolutely, number-one problem of most homes is clutter. The time before listing is the perfect opportunity to have a garage sale or donate to charity.

Box up personal treasures and non-essentials. You are going to have to do it eventually for your move, so might as well start early. Label carefully, and neatly stow them in the attic, basement, or garage, or rent a storage unit. Keep in mind that each box removed from your home means greater buyer appeal and therefore more money in your pocket. (Yes, buyers will look in your garage.)

Collections of, well, anything, do not add designer interest. A buyer is never interested or impressed by a collection.

Rooms look larger with minimal detail to distract the eye, and the good news is, there will be less stuff to collect dust.

Remove all traces of decorative styles of bygone eras. This includes Santa Fe, country, bohemian, and just about anything from the '70s or '80s. Simple, updated traditional and contemporary interiors are the best. A duplex I tried to show was so darkly Goth and foreboding my buyer wouldn't budge past the entryway. It was scary.

For those of you with children, organization can be especially challenging. Please don't say to yourself, or your agent that "buyers will just have to understand that children live here." No, they won't. However, there are neat and clean homes with children, then there are messy, war-zone homes that make buyers so anxious they can't wait to leave. Discount stores sell big storage bins that are great for toys. Try them.

Clean, scrub, and clean some more. Smoke stains on fireplace stone can be removed with muriatic acid (follow instructions since it is very toxic). Vinegar is great for mold/stains on marble and limestone. Check online for treatment suggestions.

Fix every little drip and squeaky door. Against better judgment, I let a homeowner show their home to prospects. They used their leaky tub right before the appointment. The buyers stepped over their drip bucket in the downstairs hallway, and ran out the front door.

Test every curtain and blind to ensure they operate easily. Window treatments falling to the floor when touched is not impressive. I still have a scar on my head from an old, heavy venetian blind that fell when I tried to let in sunlight.

Tricky, sticky entry locks are a pain for agents, and another red alert to buyers, indicating deferred maintenance.

Better to put valuables in a safe or a safe deposit box until you are settled in your new home. If you try to hide them, you run the risk of forgetting where you put them, which happens more often than not. I have spent hours with frantic sellers looking for jewelry they hid prior to a showing.

Secure all prescription drugs. As agents, we try to accompany clients and agents into each room, but sometimes it is impossible.

Collect owner's manuals and instruction booklets for appliances and systems, ready to pass on to new owners. You will probably run across quite a few as you clean out drawers and cabinets.

Most safety codes require smoke alarms in the bedrooms and hallways. Check your city's requirements and make sure you conform. It is also a good idea to look for safety violations such as rickety stairs or stairs without railings. Easy fixes like these may save you problems and money later.

Pack up family photographs. Each room should be as generic as possible. You want buyers to project themselves in your home, not feel like they are a guest in yours. Most rooms could benefit by having about 50 percent less art on the walls. Clear wall space is inviting.

Removing area rugs from wood floors will make rooms look larger and showcase the floors.

You may think the following goes without saying, but you would be surprised. Take down all nude or sexually explicit photographs and paintings. I do not care how artistic they are. Children will be touring your home. Hide, really hide, all sex-related toys, lotions, and magazines. Mirrors over a bed should be taken down and discarded along with red satin sheets. Showing condos to one darling young lady from the Midwest who came to the area to pursue acting, we went into a bedroom where a half naked man lounged on red satin sheets. Her mother snatched her out of there and out of Los Angeles like a lightning bolt. I do not know what the seller was thinking. Well, I do, but it was inappropriate.

Get rid of all drug paraphernalia, including marijuana, and please refrain from smoking pot inside until your house sells. Room spray can only mask so much. I had one bachelor client who proudly displayed his HIV test results. This is not classy either.

Another touchy subject involves religious material. If you are sure that the buyers looking at your home will appreciate your religious art or symbolism, then you should be fine. However, if you live in a multi-cultural area, be sensitive. Scaling back on religious décor will make buyers feel more comfortable.

One expensive estate I showed had a twenty-foot-tall gold Buddha in the living room that was so distracting my clients couldn't concentrate on the house. Worse, one seller rudely reprimanded us for not removing our shoes when we peeked into a maid's room set up as a temple to Ganesh.

After de-cluttering and organizing, step back and enter every room as if you are a picky buyer. Better yet, pretend your mother is coming to visit. Is it neat, clean, coordinated, and pretty? Maybe you need to put mismatched or odd pieces of furniture in storage. Or try matching slipcovers (plastic slipcovers are never inviting—take them off for all showings). Have the carpets and drapes cleaned, wash the windows, and paint. We only get one chance at first impressions.

Rooms that are crowded with furniture appear smaller than they are. The same is true if the furniture is too large for the room. Try to keep the scale of the furniture in correlation with the space. Small rooms need small furniture. If your king-size bed fills your bedroom, trade it out for a queen until your house sells.

If a smoker lives in your home, make them quit. Just kidding (sort of), but at least be sure all ashtrays and trashcans are emptied before you leave. Spray every surface with room deodorizer, and leave a bottle of spray and candles for your agent to use before showings. Electronic room purifiers are a big help too. Even if there are no smokers, your nose is probably used to your home's aromas, so just assume your home could benefit from fresh-smelling air.

I'll go out on a limb and assume everyone knows that the following should be discarded or properly stored without exception: last year's Christmas lights, underwear (clean or dirty), animal trophies, and cars parked on the lawn. I'm not judging, just warning.

The condition of your bathrooms and kitchen will either add value, or cost you dearly. They have to be spotless and inviting. In the bath, organize daily grooming kits so they can easily be hidden when you leave home. Clear and clean countertops are essential, and please get in the habit of closing the toilet lid.

Kitchens show best with only one small appliance on the counter, if any at all. Never leave dirty dishes out or in the sink, and avoid cooking anything that creates a strong odor while your home is on the market, especially the night before an open house. You are going to hate to hear this, but you really should organize and clean the inside of your cabinets. Serious buyers will open them. Take down everything on your refrigerator. Yes, everything.

One bug usually means there are more, so if you see one, investigate and eradicate. It only takes one roach or spider to run off a squeamish buyer.

Creating a beautiful arena is especially important in markets where agents use lockboxes. In my area it is customary for listing agents to meet buyers and their agents at the property. This gives us a chance to straighten up, turn on lights, open curtains, play music, and light candles. Where lockboxes are used, buyers will be walking in the front door cold.

Once your home is ready to show, take a practice run as a buyer. Your instincts will be the same as theirs, but they will notice if your light switches are dirty. Always leave your home neat and clean in preparation for last-minute showings. You know if you don't, that will be the day a hot buyer has to get in. Please be ready.

Besides giving sellers plenty of notice, I have learned the hard way to call before showings and sound an alarm as I enter. Still, I have been surprised by sleeping homeowners. One of my clients only got out of bed for showings. Do not rely on your agent to be your alarm. Or your maid. Are you listening, bachelors?

Sympathize with the housekeepers. If you are lucky enough to have one, think about giving them a little bonus for taking extra care while your home is on the market. It is exhausting keeping a home perfect.

"It's called a screwdriver. I will be happy to show you how it works."

THAT'S IT? THERE MUST BE MORE TO IT

Just like a dysfunctional relationship, you may not want to hear criticism about your home or take advice on how to improve it. But if you are sensing that it still could use some work, here are some ideas for upgrading and staging that will add value.

Floors are really, really important. Professional carpet cleaners that use a truck-mounted system are great, but if there are still spots and stains, it is time for a new action plan. You can remove the carpet and re-finish the wood floors underneath, or replace the carpet. No, emphatically no, buyers will not want you to leave it as is and let them choose their own carpet. They will consider your home a "fixer" in need of improvements and offer you less. True, credit for carpet seems like a great idea at the beginning of a listing. However it usually gets negotiated out during counter-offers. Better to choose a neutral color and eliminate the deferred maintenance.

Wood floors are preferred over carpet by most people. Throw rugs need to be clean and in good condition. Do not try staining a cement slab and calling it finished. Concrete floors are fabulous if done by a designer in a showcase; they look cold and cheap when done by most homeowners.

Bathrooms and kitchens are where improvements are most appreciated and will make you money. Marble and granite countertop are wonderful. If you have tile, make sure the grout sparkles or re-grout. If you decide to re-tile, some of the new ceramic ones are gorgeous and reasonably priced, as are travertine and slate. Make sure the grout matches well. Even expensive tile can look cheap if the grout has too much of a contrast.

Check the caulking around the tub, shower, and toilet. Extremely worn tile, sinks, and tubs can get a quick, inexpensive facelift by having them glazed. Most companies that specialize in this will guarantee the surfaces for a few years, which is a nice value to pass on to your buyers. Another option is to cover wall tile with paneling.

Granite, marble, and stone composite countertops are available at reasonable prices, even pre-fabricated for standard-size vanities. Now they also offer a thin granite overlay that covers existing tops, eliminating demo.

Worn, dated, or chronically leaky faucets should be replaced. Using the same manufacturer's products, even shower controls are easy to install. If the plumbing proves too difficult, an option is to have the faucet trim re-plated. There is a wide variety of metal choices, and fixtures can look new for a fraction of the cost.

Sellers should become familiar with local retrofit ordinances. You may be required to replace toilets with low-flow models. Besides uncovering what costs a buyer might ask you to incur, if you have to buy new toilets, why not do it now?

Refinish or replace dated light fixtures. New cabinet pulls and towel rods/hooks can upgrade a bath tremendously.

In baths, add fluffy towels, matching rugs, scented candles, and a bottle of bubble bath. You will wish you had done this years ago.

The quickest, most inexpensive ways to spruce up dated kitchens is to lay down new flooring and have appliances painted. There are wonderful low-end flooring choices too, such as cork, coated fabrics, and sisal-looking vinyl. Professional-looking stainless appliances are still preferable if you are replacing yours. Cabinet depth refrigerators are a good choice to give you more room. Browse manufacturer showrooms or supplier sales for quality at a discount and package deals.

Good kitchen countertop alternatives include wood, stainless steel, ceramic tile, or a combination of materials. The new laminates are reasonable and come in great colors. One of my listings had a designer kitchen with concrete counters topped by thick tempered glass. My favorite material is quartz composite for simplicity, uniformity, and practicality. Recently I watched a demonstration on how to resurface worn laminate countertops that looked easy.

Worn cabinets can be renewed with paint, stain, or car wax. Accessorize with new pulls (and new hinges if you take the doors off to paint). For more of an upgrade, reface with new cabinet doors.

Drop ceilings with fluorescent lights really date kitchens. I suggest replacing them with recessed cans or new light fixtures. Usually the ceilings can be easily finished in the raised area, which will add height and interest and make the room appear larger.

Bedrooms need to be relaxing and inviting. Dress the beds with elegant linens. Aim for simple and sophisticated. Refer to home furnishing catalogs for ideas. If you don't want to buy new linens, starch and press the top layers so they look new. Organize closets, add pillows, scented candles, and slippers.

All rooms need to be lightly accessorized so they don't look bare or cold. You will be surprised how much warmth one pillow will add. Instead of art on a wall, try a mirror.

The most desirable feature that will add value to your home is sunlight. If your home is naturally light, fabulous. Trim plants away from windows to allow in even more. For homes with dark rooms that can't be corrected with white paint and mirrors, solar tube skylights make a huge difference. The raised plastic domes catch sunlight on your roof and send it down mirrored shafts into your home. Professional installers or contractors can pop them in your roof in two to four hours with minimal mess or disturbance. More sunlight also means less need for lighting, so you will be adding a green component that can be highlighted among your home's features.

Speaking of lighting, replace bulbs with the brightest ones possible. Dimmers help set the mood for night showings, but buyers like to clearly see into every nook and cranny. How old are your light fixtures? Stores sell ones that are nice looking yet inexpensive. Energy efficient bulbs and fixtures further the green effort, but the chief goal is to look updated. Cheap-but-new trumps expensive-but-dated in almost every situation.

Doubting a feature in your home? Invite a few friends over and ask them to be brutally honest about it. This may be painful, but it could open the door to increased profit. We all get accustomed to our surroundings and cease to be objective.

A fireplace made of ugly stone? Paint it, cover it, or replace it if your friends think it will dramatically improve your home. In some instances, a new mantel can be introduced to disguise and distract.

Sniff around for must or mold. Look for leaks and hire someone to crawl under your house to make sure nothing is dripping. If you smell it, buyers will smell it. Home inspectors most certainly will find it. You do not want to sell your house at a depressed price because buyers think there is deferred maintenance. Most plumbers or contractors can fix water problems and know how to eradicate mold. Bleach and water can tackle light mold. Look online for remedies.

At the very least, be prepared. If you do not want to fix a problem now, get a couple of estimates on how much it will cost. This is especially true for major items like a new roof. Then you will know what to expect if asked to credit the buyer after inspections, should it prove to be a breaking point. Always get three estimates. Always. One week I got an estimate to repair my sewer for $15,000. The next week I actually got the whole thing replaced by a reasonable plumber for $2,500.

Sometimes it is smart to have a termite inspection before you list. Dry rot is much cheaper to repair when done by a carpenter of your choice. This is because if it gets noted in an inspection report and handed to the buyer, estimates from termite companies usually include subbing out the carpentry.

When infestation allows, I recommend hiring green companies. They use an environmentally correct borax solution that dries up the critters and does not disrupt your life, or knock off your weather vane. They guarantee their work just like tent fumigation companies, are just as thorough, and are less expensive.

Look up at your ceilings. High-end builders do not use textured spray. Scraping it off is a messy job, but it can drastically update rooms and add sophistication. Homes built before 1978 could have texture that contains asbestos. In that case, test it and call a professional remover. Other solutions include plastering over it or encapsulating it with drywall. Handymen can quickly remove uncontaminated cottage cheese-type ceilings. They cover the floor with plastic, wear long sleeves, safety goggles, and face mask, then attack with a spray water bottle and spatula. I have done it myself, but I certainly will never do it again.

This may seem picky, but outdated light switches set a tone for the whole house. I always switch out the old small lever type with the newer wide, flat ones.

Building codes usually require that all electrical outlets near a water source, like in the kitchen, baths, garage and on the exterior must be ground fault circuit interrupting (GFCI). Conforming now will save you time later.

Not handy or inclined? Your Realtor© may be willing to help coordinate outside workers. In my area skilled handymen charge around thirty-five dollars per hour plus materials. They can roll through repairs quickly if you have a list prepared.

Every project you complete will add value and desirability to your home, but beware not to over-improve. If the homes in your neighborhood have laminate countertops, no need to invest in granite.

Another warning: be careful not to undertake too many projects at once. I have met with many frazzled sellers who began knocking out projects, got overwhelmed, and had to hire professionals to finish. This usually ends up costing more than it would if you had hired them in the first place. Not to mention the enormous disruption to household harmony.

Define your rooms with furniture and rugs, making the formal rooms elegant. Dining rooms should have a chandelier, 30" above the table.

Besides defining room use, the strategic placement of furniture and accessories can distract from imperfections. Hide that ugly corner with a plant! Turn that unusual alcove into a reading nook! Know your market. Who is buying in your neighborhood? This will determine whether a spare room should be set up as a nursery or an office.

If your home is outdated, staging with contemporary furniture can create the illusion of a newer home. Sometimes simply re-arranging furniture can make a home appear larger.

Vacant homes really should be staged. An empty room is never inviting. Furthermore, believe it or not, some people have a hard time recognizing rooms for what they are intended. Unless there is a dining table in the dining room, they are confused. This is especially true for homes with open/flexible floor plans and awkwardly shaped rooms.

The National Association of Realtors© offers affordable staging tips on their web site if you decide to tackle staging yourself. Some of the furniture rental companies have designers that will help you select and arrange furniture for free.

When looking for a professional stager, interview several. Most companies will work with you on the cost, and some will let you pay the balance out of escrow. Do not get stressed if you are clueless or overwhelmed. Some of my clients have gotten relief and beneficial advice by hiring a designer for an in-home consultation.

Ignore this advice and you will sell your property. But, could it have sold sooner or for more? Staged properties sell faster and at a higher price than vacant ones. All of this effort will pay off, I promise. Pretty homes sell faster than ugly ones. Your home will especially stand out amongst all of the neglected foreclosures.

"Of course it's a mess, it's a foreclosure. However, it is in your price range."

THE PRETTIEST HOUSE ON THE BLOCK

Buyers' eyes light up when they see a beautifully landscaped yard, making them predisposed to love the house before they even get out of the car. Putting time into your yard will be worthwhile. Some designers are genius at curb appeal. If you are not, you can get a high impact by just doing all of those outdoor chores you have put off. For example, say goodbye to every plant that is dead, leggy, or overgrown. Trim overgrown hedges or trees early so they will have time to sprout new growth. Remove every leaf that is blocking light into your windows. Make sure all the sprinklers work. Clean the gutters.

Keep your lawn manicured. Reseed or disguise bare ground patches. If that is impossible, make it look like a planned feature. Boulders strategically placed with ground cover or pebbles around the base work great. Synthetic grass is an option. Or try a fountain or bird bath, but don't add statuary unless you own a huge estate.

Landscaping trends change over the years, so discover what the builders are planting now and copy it. Drive around high-end neighborhoods to get ideas. Sellers living in drought areas will win points by choosing plants that are conservation smart.

Every view out of your windows should be pretty. Plus a view out of a window will expand the room. (If this is impossible, try sheer drapes or hang a basketful of flowers just outside.) If you have an unsightly view from the yard, explore options. Build a fence, add a trellis, or plant a hedge. Bamboo is extremely fast growing. Or find something to distract from it, like a beautiful flower bed or well lit tree. Even large expanses of boring wall can be magically transformed with bougainvillea.

Privacy in the backyard is a valuable asset. One of my listings had vicious pit bulls next door. We named them "Damn-it" and "Shut-up." Not only were the snarling beasts loud, they sat perched on a raised balcony within clear view of the listed home's kitchen, living room, and backyard. Mothers grabbed their babies and raced out of the house. I tried a silent bark deterrent to get them quiet, but that only worked for about a week. The seller eventually understood the importance of hiding the dogs, and built a solid fence. As soon as the dogs could not see into the yard, they quit barking. The house sold soon after.

In recent years outdoor living spaces have tremendously added enjoyment and value to properties. If you are not utilizing your yard, look for ways to be creative. It can be as simple as a chair and book on a balcony or a swing on a porch, or as elaborate as an outdoor living room and kitchen.

Pool and spa areas should be inviting and alluring, down to rolled towels on lounge chairs and magazines on a side table. Don't crowd decks, porches, and patios, or they will appear small.

Patch, paint, and clean the exterior of the house. Power washers can make brick and stone look new, but they can also blow old stucco apart, so be careful. They work wonders for renewing walkways, driveways, and garage floors.

For goodness sake take down burglar bars. At least take down the bars that are visible from the street or when approaching the front door. All they do is advertise how unsafe your neighborhood is. If you are insecure, you have options. One choice is a burglar alarm. Most companies will install it for free if you sign up for a year of monitoring—one more way to add good value. An alternative is to hire a metal fabricator to make guards that complement your home's style. This is a little tricky since bars have to be operable inside bedrooms, but it adds character if there aren't bedrooms on the front of the house. I have seen some beautiful custom guards that are especially charming on Spanish and Mediterranean homes. At the very, very least, paint burglar bars white or the same color as the house so they don't stand out.

Take down signage that is not welcoming. Buyers do not want to beware of dog or enter at their own risk, and rarely will they share your sense of humor.

Clean walkways and make sure they are level. You do not want buyers tripping on the way to the front door. Spruce up the mailbox and house numbers. The sound of water from a fountain near the front door is wonderful, especially if you live on a busy street.

I have never met an inspector who didn't love to exaggerate drainage problems. So if you have one, remedy it as best you can.

Should budget allow and your garage door is an older model, replacing it can greatly improve your curb appeal. My area is inundated with ads for new doors for as little as $399. You will be amazed how much a new door will improve the look of your home. Newer doors are installed with a safety check that prevents them from closing on pets or children. This is a great feature to pass on, and it may be required by code.

An important outdoor factor you have absolutely no control over is your neighbors. Nobody wants to buy next door to an eyesore. If this is a problem, look for ways to mitigate the situation like a privacy fence or hedge. Sometimes a little act of kindness such as mowing your neighbor's yard or watering a flowerbed can greatly help. The house across the street from mine is bright orange. The trim on the house is red brick which makes the orange look even worse. I am considering asking the nice owners to let me paint the front a neutral cream. This will look sophisticated, especially from my side of the street. I don't want to offend them, but it may be worth a try.

Watch for neglected foreclosures or abandoned houses. Besides being unsightly, they can attract vagrants and vandals. If there are any near you, try to organize the neighbors to tend the yard so it looks maintained and occupied. Many banks are so overwhelmed they can't manage all the properties. You want your street, as well as your house, to be as desirable as possible.

"It is a buyer's market, you know. You may want to re-think these black walls."

COLOR ME FABULOUS

Yes, I actually had a client who painted his bedroom walls black. That particular room was gorgeous. The black walls and glossy, ebony wood floors were contrasted by white shag rugs, baseboards, crown moldings, and art deco-style wall trim. Crystal chandeliers, wall sconces, mirrors, and candles added sparkle. The seller is a fabulous designer. Nevertheless, as pretty as it was, the first thing the buyers did was paint the room beige.

Unless you are a designer or have designer help, resist the urge to be creative or artistic in your color choices. Bright colors are subjective and risky. Dark colors are gloomy and make rooms appear smaller.

Choose a light, neutral color. Colors intensify when they go on four walls, and they reflect the color of the floor, so test a few. Buy quarts and paint large patches on a couple of walls. Let them dry and use two coats so you are evaluating the finished color. I sometimes test colors by painting eight-by-eleven-inch pieces of paper so they can be easily moved around on different walls to see how the light plays against them.

Do not think buyers will be able to visualize your rooms in different colors. Most likely they will not. This surprised me too, but many people cannot imagine a room with change. Even a suggestion of "picture this room with white walls" is met with blank stares. Clueless.

This also means that you should not avoid painting because you assume buyers will want to choose their own colors. This, like new carpet, is not true. Buyers do not want to have to paint their new home unless they are looking for a fixer. If that is the case, they will discount the value of your home. Keep in mind that paint is the cheapest, most effective way to add value.

Do not paint each room a different color unless you have a 7,500-square-foot Mediterranean estate. If you stick to one color, the rooms will flow together and your home will seem larger. If you want to vary it, at least keep all the colors in the same palette, or select different hues of the same color. If you have to be artistic, choose one wall in one room to be the accent and paint it more boldly than the rest. If it doesn't work, try again. Paint is cheap.

Sorry, sports fans, most people will not appreciate game rooms painted in your team's colors. At the very, very least, offer to paint the room white before you close escrow.

Traditional or non-descript rooms evolve into sophisti-cated beauties with crown moldings. Inexpensive, composite, pre-primed, and even flexible ones are readily available. Paint crowns and baseboards white, and walls khaki or beige for instant elegance.

If the ceilings are a lighter shade than the walls, it will give the illusion of height. My favorite color combo is flat off-white for the ceilings, light beige for the walls, and glossy bright white for the trim. You can always add color with a pillow or towels.

Wallpaper is making a comeback. It is cropping up in small rooms of multi-million dollar designer showcases. However it is such a personal choice I certainly do not recommend it. In fact, if your home has wallpaper that was installed more than five years ago, it probably should be taken down. This is especially true if it is a floral or busy pattern.

If you love the color of the walls in your home and do not want to paint, at least scrub them and touch up the scuffed areas. If the new paint and old paint don't exactly match, apply a light coat of paint that has been thinned with water. You will be "washing" the walls. The smell of fresh paint is as intoxicating to buyers as vanilla candles.

The thrill of new paint pertains to the exterior of your home as well. Most paint companies offer brochures with suggestions of beautiful exterior color schemes. A word of caution: if your home is close to neighbors, eyeball it with their colors in mind. Three beige houses in a row could diminish the sophistication. And your lovely grey could appear purple next to your neighbor's blue-grey. Make yours the prettiest house on the block.

"Just because you throw a tarp over it doesn't mean it isn't there."

ISN'T ANYBODY LISTENING!

OK, I get it. You do not have a dime to spend on prepping your house. In that case, here are the bare necessities that only cost elbow grease.

- First, throw out the junk, have a garage sale, donate to charity.

- Box up items you can live without for six months. Organize closets and drawers.

- Take down most of the art on the walls, and pack away photos.

- Repair everything in need, especially plumbing drips. Check the smoke alarms.

- Make sure all of your light bulbs are working and are maximum wattage.

- Take down worn or dated window coverings wherever you can live with exposed windows.

- Scrub everything. Walls, floors, tile, windows, light fixtures—everything.

- Wash and starch bed linens. If they are dingy, dye them a rich color.

- Outside, remove all dead brush and repair anything that you can fix with a hammer and nails or screwdriver. If anything is unsightly, remove it, camouflage it, or distract from it. As a last resort, cover it with a new tarp. Trim back all brush blocking light into the windows. Reseed, kill weeds, fertilize. Plant flowers around the front door.

- If you can't afford "breathtaking," aim for "friendly."

- If something is in disrepair, at the very least, stop further deterioration.

These are the same criteria that banks address when they take over foreclosed properties. Step one is cleaning, and hauling all debris and personal property left behind by previous occupants. Next is property preservation such as stopping leaks, fixing drips, killing termites, etc. Lastly, if time and budget warrant, make improvements. This is the order in which you need to spend time, money, and energy in preparing your property for sale.

Take a deep breath and know that you have done a great job in getting your home ready for the next family.

"Oh, you have cats? I didn't notice."

HERE, FLORENCE!

For some homes, there isn't enough deodorizing spray in the world to mask bad odors. I am particularly referring to those with cats.

I like cats. Some cats. However, they make me sneeze and litter boxes stink. I know I am not alone in this opinion. Even if there are only 10 percent of buyers who share my view, that's too many for home sellers to chance.

Do not for one moment think that putting the litter box in the shower or bathtub erases the odor. And, yes, buyers always look in tubs and showers.

Besides, do you really think your cat is going to love having hundreds of strangers parading through their territory? I showed one property where the cat was so freaked she ran out of the door the minute it opened and didn't come home until the middle of the night. It was a fun afternoon walking through the neighborhood yelling, "Florence! Here, Florence!" The sellers were not happy.

If waiting for that one cat lover who relates to the smell, isn't allergic, and will make you an offer, you may be waiting a long time. Loan Flo to your mom until your house sells. At the very least, take Florence with you, spray every surface with odor-eliminator, and put the litter box in the garage for all showings.

Dogs can be a problem too. Besides the hair and smell, some people are just terrified of dogs. All dogs. Even little fur balls that are the cutest things on earth. This fear can keep otherwise reasonable buyers from getting out of the car, no matter how pretty the house is from the driveway. The basis of this fear stems from personal experience to cultural conditioning, but it is real and cannot be assuaged by Realtors©.

You may be thinking, "This won't apply to me. My dog is perfectly behaved." Oh really? Have you seen how your pet acts when you are gone? Do you know how your dog will act with strangers in their house? More often than not, they will behave badly.

Badly behaved dogs fall into three groups. The growling, snarling dog in the corner who looks rabid and shakes with anger; the barking, yipping dog that snaps at ankles and follows buyers room to room; and my favorite, the lover dog who likes to hump legs. Let me tell you, buyers are not amused, and agents will avoid showing your house.

You and your pet need to be absent for showings and open houses. Try doggie day camp, or, at the very least, make arrangements with your agent to put your dog in a run or portable kennel until the buyers leave. Frequent baths help, too. Currently I have a listing with two canine family members. Being a dedicated agent, on occasion I have picked them up before a showing, taken them to my house, and then gone back to meet the buyers. So far it has worked well for all.

Do I really have to warn anybody about the perils of having snakes for pets? If so, you probably do not have many women visitors. Invite a few over and see what happens when they notice the snake. The same applies in a lesser way to ferrets, piranhas, and lizards, all of which I have encountered as pets. You cannot afford to eliminate women or sissies from your buyer pool.

Most people like fish. However, beware, if a fish is going to die, it will do so right before a showing. Maybe fish get nervous with extra activity in the house. Who knows? But don't blame your Realtor© if your fish dies. Just thank us for scooping it out and throwing it away before buyers arrive. (OK, sometimes we bury fish in the garden, but you get the point.)

I hate to bring up the topic of tenants under pets. However, if you are selling a property that is occupied by tenants, I encourage you to offer them some sort of incentive to cooperate with showings. Even if they say there is no problem, more than likely they will not keep the place sparkling.

Bitter spouses forced to sell their homes due to divorce fall into another category entirely. The clever ways I have seen them sabotage deals by leaving the property in a disgusting condition for showings is almost commendable. Hopefully all parties involved will support you in your quest for a quick sale.

Also under the category of pets, please warn all of your family and friends that you are selling. If they have keys to your home, remind them to pick up after themselves. It is a good idea to have a designated spot to post the schedule of open houses and showings. Besides walking in on a man in the shower, I almost had a heart attack when the Hare Krishna son of a seller quietly stepped out of a closet when the house was supposedly vacant. I still jump at the sight of orange robes.

The bottom line is, try to keep all your pets, friends, relatives, and children curbed until your house sells.

"Don't you have any bigger signs?"

MARCHING BANDS WON'T HELP, EITHER

Skywriting, like other expensive advertising, will not generate more money for your house. It may help with exposure, but don't count on a buyer offering you a creative marketing bonus.

Don't get me wrong, I love, love, love big glossy ads with my name associated with gorgeous homes. But really, save your money. In fact, in my market the homes that are over-priced do the most overkill advertising. Realistically, advertising announces your arrival to the market, but your price is what entices real buyers in the door and wins you an offer.

Do many buyers view your home without their own agent? If this is true in your area, then run consistent advertising aimed at buyers and hold public open houses.

The most advantageous, critical place to advertise your property is on the Internet. It is important for these sites to be easily located and have good pictures. Have your agent set up a specific web site for your property featured in your local multiple listing service (MLS).

In a majority of markets, serious home buyers also rely on their agents. For these cities the most productive advertising is targeted at agents. This includes email flyers sent to agents, print ads in broker and real estate magazines, post cards, print flyers, and office announcements.

Buyers relocating from other markets and countries now shop easily online for homes. So save your money earmarked for foreign newspapers. Many agents working with buyers set up automated alerts, so as soon as new listings hit the MLS, the information is e-mailed directly to qualified buyers.

Jot down copy ideas that best describe your home to share with your agent. Be concise and accurate. In most markets a full bath means those with tubs. A three-quarter bath has a shower, and a half bath or powder room has a toilet and sink. Eclectic and Bohemian are not architectural styles. Do not call your home updated unless it has been done so within the last five to ten ears. Do not call your home remodeled unless you have recently completed the project. Avoid adjectives such as "cozy" and "quaint" or any other word that implies small.

It is fun to look through the home sections of the paper and to read the slick home magazines, but most firms advertise primarily to attract new clients to their agency, not to sell specific homes. With the lag time print advertising requires, many homes could be in escrow before the ad runs. In some markets newspapers and home magazines can still be an asset, especially if they have an online version, but print in general is losing readers rapidly. The magazines that are in correlation with the local multiple listing services are more accurate than other publications.

Most Realtors© send out e-mail flyers to agents, but old-fashioned paper flyers in the front yard work well in some neighborhoods. Yard signs that direct drive-by lookers to web sites or information recordings are an option. If rude buyers or agents drive by your house, see the sign, and decide to knock on the door, do not let them in. Serious lookers will make an appointment for another time.

Smart agents love Sunday open houses because they can pick up buyers who roam in without agent representation. I hate public open houses. First, all the nosy neighbors come through and offer suggestions or criticism. Then in come the set decorators and designers who saw the ads and want to check it out. Sunday opens are free entertainment for home improvement nuts, and don't forget the family who just needs to use the bathroom. I know from firsthand experience open houses are golden opportunities for thieves. They blend in with the guests, act interested, then split up to privately look for treasure.

Sometimes thieves come to opens to case houses for future burglaries. If your property is vacant, do not leave anything valuable and easy to remove, like flat-screen TVs. Thieves are fast and can break in, remove the goods, and be gone before the alarm company can warn you of the intrusion. This happened to one of my vacant listings. The house was cased during a Sunday open and robbed a week later on a holiday night around eleven o'clock. The thieves even knew the house was watched by neighbors who went to bed around ten-thirty. Consider staging the home to make it appear to be occupied by adding toiletries in the bath and linens on the bed.

Homes need to be readily available for buyers to see. Fortunately for me, in my area real buyers have agents who preview homes for them, then schedule appointments. Follow the practices that are common for your area.

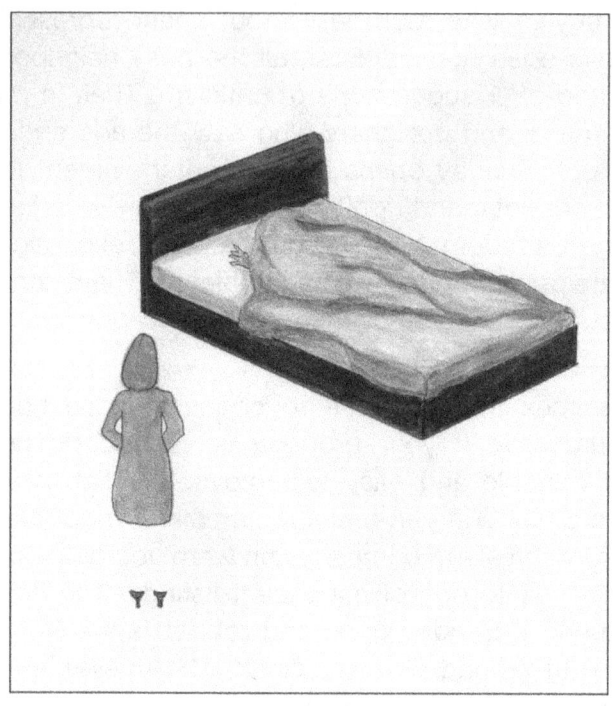

"Alright, pull the covers over your head and I'll let you know when the buyers leave."

LEAVE ME ALONE

One afternoon I arrived to show a home and one of my sellers was still in bed. Her husband was at work, her kids were at school, and she could not quite face the day. It is called depression. It happens often to home sellers, especially if the bank is looming at the front door. As a friend all I could do was tell her it would eventually be alright. As a Realtor© all I could do was tell her to pull the covers over her head and I would let her know when the buyers left.

Selling a home is stressful. Moving to a new home is stressful. Having to live with stress while keeping your home neat and clean all the time is beyond stressful. Please be aware of the pressure you are under. If you live with anyone else, be sensitive to the stress they are feeling as well. No sale is more valuable than your relationship. Many divorces spring out of buying or selling property. The best advice I could ever give a buyer or seller is to be nice to your loved ones during the process.

Seller's remorse is real. So is buyer's remorse. You will have that day when you wake up and think "what have I done!" Sometimes a little case of remorse escalates to panic. Try to breathe and remember that what you are feeling is normal. If it doesn't subside, talk it over with your partner and Realtor©. My boss used to hand out pill bottles filled with candy to her clients marked "For Seller's Remorse, take one a day until it passes."

Do not act on your friend's advice. Sorry, but rarely do friends face the exact same circumstances. You are vulnerable to bad advice when under the spell of remorse. I have seen friends and family spoil many deals, robbing clients of good choices and in some cases, robbing them of huge equity earnings.

Also remember that this feeling of remorse will probably hit you and your partner at different times throughout the process. Usually, as soon as you are calm and set on moving forward, your partner will wake up in a panic. Better yet, as soon as both of you are calm, the people buying your home will panic. This too is normal. All of us have those days when we don't want to get out of bed.

"I know what my condo is worth! Don't show me those comps again!"

THE DREADED REDUCTION

Besides winning a listing, the hardest thing for a Realtor© to do is get sellers to reduce. The conversation is akin to insulting mothers. We know it is hard, but sometimes it is necessary.

Especially in this recession, it is extremely difficult to predict the market value of your home. One can only make an educated guess and test the market. After awhile if you do not have offers, reduce.

Too few lookers mean that ready buyers and agents think your home is too overpriced to consider. If you have many lookers but no offers, your home does not compare well to others in the same price range. A long pause in lookers signals a reduction is needed.

Tracking the activity on your home is a good visual way to analyze your pricing. Keep a calendar or log with showings and opens. Even in a slow and downward market, there are qualified buyers. To attract them, it is critical to stay aggressively priced. You will notice the number of showings increase with each reduction. If the market is still falling where you live, and you reduce in small increments, you may not be reducing fast enough to catch a buyer. This is called chasing the market, and it can cost you dearly.

Unhappy with the response you are getting? It is the price, not your Realtor©. Change your price, not your Realtor©. You are the conductor; your agent is just shoveling fuel.

Ask your agent what is the main objection that buyers have with your home. If it is easily correctable, it may be more resourceful to correct than reduce. For example, if your bedroom suffers with traffic noise, replacing the windows could be more cost efficient than reducing. (Window manufacturers are now making triple-paned windows for maximum noise reduction. Retrofit windows can be popped in over the old metal frames so stucco and siding demolition is not necessary.)

A big reduction is not always necessary. Just enough to make a difference in the buyer pool, or push buyers to get off the fence and make an offer. Think of it as an excuse to advertise something new and have another open house for brokers. Your agent will coach you on the timing of the reduction and the amount. Go ahead, push.

"You can start signing the disclosures. I'll get coffee."

I KNOW NOTHING

How annoying is it to ask a Realtor© how big a house is, and they answer three bedrooms and two baths? I know, I know. We are trained to answer that way. If we do quote square feet, we must give our source. As an agent, it is drummed into our heads not to make any claims about property. You have seen the disclaimers on the bottom of ads and flyers: we cannot guarantee the data, only pass on information. My office even has a disclosure that I call the "I know nothing form." Clients have to sign an acknowledgement that the agents are not responsible for originating or verifying data. Better to be annoying than to get sued for quoting an erroneous description.

As a seller, you should also to be careful about what specifics you pass on to prospective buyers. Never say "exactly." Do not stand by your fence and point to the property line unless you just had it surveyed. Do not measure your square footage and give your buyer a tally. What if you are off six inches? In past court cases, buyers have been awarded monetary damages for the discrepancy.

That error can be costly. For example, if you advertise your home as being 4,000 square feet, and you sell it for $500,000, that averages $125 per square foot. If later the house is measured at 3,500 square feet, the buyers could claim that they should be reimbursed for 500 square feet at $125, or $62,500. It has happened. And, no, the garage cannot be counted in total square feet.

It is safer to quote outside sources, like the bank appraiser, the tax assessor, or the builder. Better yet, let the buyer hire an expert to verify dimensions. This shifts the responsibility and liability away from you.

On the other side of the white picket fence, as a seller you are responsible for disclosing everything you know that may impact your property. Do not for a minute think you should not. Even slight exclusions can come back years later to bite you in the form of a lawsuit. This is especially true in a bad economy. It is better to take the chance that a disclosure could sour the deal, than it is to hide a defect.

Buyers can sue you for anything, even frivolous things. They may not win, but who needs the aggravation? There was a lawsuit where buyers sued the sellers because they did not know that the trees on the property would drop their leaves in fall. I am not kidding. That is why in my state we disclose everything, assuming no one has any common sense.

Included in the blanket small print are such things as, if you buy near a golf course, you may find a golf ball in your yard. If you buy near an airport, you may hear airplane noise. Now we have to disclose if we know the property ever housed the manufacture of methamphetamines. None of my clients has ever been a party to this, but it is good to know if you stand the chance of police ramming down your door by mistake, among other things.

One house I sold is in an area regulated by the Coastal Commission, the official committee that regulates California coastal areas. The seller inadvertently put three little steps a wee bit too close to an oak tree that is covered by an endangered species act. A Coastal Commission member went on the property, saw the violation, fined the seller ten thousand dollars and made him plant fifty oak trees in the area. In addition, the oak tree in question had to be monitored by the commission for five years to make sure it was not damaged. Being ignorant of local laws does not protect you.

As farfetched as this is for most of us, the point is, do not think twice about disclosing the condition of your property. If bathroom tile is cracked, let everyone know the tile is cracked. You do not want a call later from the buyer telling you they did not know the tile was cracked.

I remember one seller who did not share that he had a floor safe under the dining room table that he was taking with him. Surprise! The buyers were met with a huge hole in the floor during their final walk-through. Chaos ensued.

Disclose or advise the buyers in writing. Memories get hazy after closings. The word "disclose" may imply a defect, so include an advisory on non-inflammatory issues such as underground pipelines and trash pickup times.

In most states it is the buyer's responsibility to investigate, but a seller's responsibility to divulge laws, ordinances, and requirements that affect the property. As a Realtor©, we can help you deliver reports to the buyer. If your buyer is planning on cutting down a protected oak tree in order to put in a pool, better to disclose before escrow.

I even advise buyers to do chimney inspections and sewer line scopes. If you are in a high-risk area, mold or radon inspections may be good. Geological inspections are usual and ordinary in California because of the hillside terrain and earth-quakes.

True, some inspectors are better than others. One of the best geological inspectors in my area calmly informs buyers new to the state that the farther you are from one fault line, the closer you are to another. In contrast, one inspector scared a wife so badly she was on the next plane back to Chicago and cancelled the deal.

Try to remain calm and keep things in perspective during inspections. Easier said than done, I know. I was party to a very expensive inspection where the inspector called out a soap dispenser that didn't work. Actually, it was out of soap. He made a big deal about nothing. As much as I wanted to rip out the soap dispenser and throw it in the buyer's face, I decided to be prudent and fill it up.

Think of buyers' inspectors as your friends. They shift the responsibility of disclosure away from you. When you sell your house, you want the door closed firmly behind you as you leave.

"And here's a guest bath..."

THEY WANT WHAT?

Here comes the hard part, negotiating an offer. I know you did not really think buyers would love your home so much they would gladly pay what you are asking. Unless you have more than one offer, buyers are going to grind.

Try to keep offers in perspective. Sleep on all your decisions. Remember the buyers are just trying to get a good deal. They are nervous. If values are falling, they are losing money before they even move in.

Look for compromise. Aim for feeling satisfied that you have done the best you can do. Having said that, buyers always think they paid too much. Sellers always think they sold too low. Those are probably signs of a fair deal.

Many buyers' agents prefer to present offers face-to-face with sellers. This allows them to tell you a little about their clients, present the terms, and answer your questions. Their dream consequence is for you to sign their offer on the spot, which rarely happens. Whether you want to sit down with these agents is entirely up to you.

If you decide to entertain the buyer's agents, do not become confrontational, no matter how insulting their offer. You want the buyer's agent to be sympathetic towards you. Politely tell them you will discuss it and get back to them. Or explain why you cannot accept such a low offer. After the agent leaves, you can hit the roof. Remember, getting the buyer's agent on your side can be financially beneficial.

I'm reminded of presenting an offer to a family years ago. As I mentioned the purchase price, the wife moaned, grabbed her chest, and fell to the floor writhing in pain. The husband angrily escorted me to the door ranting about how insulted he was. Pure theatrics, but my client and I were afraid that their behavior was indicative of how they would be throughout the entire transaction, and we withdrew the offer.

Buyers offer low purchase prices for several reasons. The easiest to understand is if they simply cannot afford any more than offered. Usually their agent will divulge this when stating their case. Some buyers will only buy a house if they feel that they are getting a deal. This usually requires back and forth negotiating. If you have a buyer that likes to play this game, it doesn't hurt to play along. Your agent will advise you on what increments to counter. These negotiations are painful, but you can arrive at a mutually accepted price. Keep your eye on the goal.

If you have a walk-away number, a true walk-away number, you can tell your agent that you refuse to look at offers under a certain price. You risk rejecting viable buyers, but you are entitled to do so. This can eliminate bottom feeders and insincere shoppers.

Don't let the little things sidetrack the negotiations. You don't have to throw in your great grandmother's chandelier. Instead consider it a compliment they want something you love and offer an alternative, or a credit. Strive for a meeting of the minds, and then back it up with paperwork.

To avoid confrontation during negotiations, it is a good idea to let your agent know from the start what items you want included in the sale, and which ones you do not. That way it can be disclosed up front. In most states, it is customary for all things attached to be included. This includes window treatments, lighting fixtures, built-in appliances, built-in furniture, and television mounts. If you are intending to take the chandelier, either disclose it in all the write-ups, or better yet, take it down and replace it with another before you list. That will eliminate any possibility of discord.

Items that are usually taken by the sellers or are negotiable include such things as flat-screen TVs, free-standing appliances, and patio flowerpots. I had some extremely unhappy buyers because they were surprised that the sellers took the fireplace tools. (Guess who bought the buyers new fireplace tools?)

In times like these, you must not be sidetracked by bad offers. Do not be so anxious to sell that you fall prey to con artists or buyers with good intentions but no money. I once had an offer on a lease from a scam artist that was almost a joke. He rolled up in a fancy car, flashing an expensive watch and shoes. This guy convinced some novice real estate agent to represent him, and there was a well-dressed friend in tow. He had big stories, made big promises, and a big offer. It was unclear as to what he did for a living. There was mention of a charity, foundation, and off-shore something. The offer got a little complicated, but he was representing a fair amount of cash, so we asked for credit reports.

His available cash in the bank was suspiciously close to the balances on the credit cards. Odds are he pulled money out of the cards to put in the bank. Then we hit the Internet. What do you know? Searching his name revealed a "Beware

Of" blog posted by past victims. If someone cheats or scams you, please post it. It really can help others.

There was an offer on one of my properties from a smarmy buyer who also put an offer on another house at the same time without informing either seller. Both offers had similar terms and coinciding time frames. Not illegal but certainly deceitful. At the very least his agent should have disclosed dual offers. The buyer was hoping to tie up both properties until he decided which to purchase. Very rarely do these boobs succeed in ripping off sellers, but they can tie up a property for months. This is costly in a falling market.

The same caution applies to honest buyers with good intentions who make offers contingent on selling their home. These are not viable offers. It amazes me that sellers who have trouble selling their own homes will accept an offer from someone who thinks they can sell theirs in a few weeks. A smarter way to go is, wait until the prospective buyer's house is solidly in escrow with no remaining contingencies. Then entertain their offer.

Also be alert to buyers whose money is going to be wired in from another country. Wires usually don't take more than forty-eight hours. Do not tie up your property for false promises. Do not accept an offer until the buyer's money can be verified. You may be missing a better offer. As Realtors© it is our fiduciary responsibility to inform and protect our clients as much as possible, but do not allow your desire to sell interfere with good judgment.

As difficult as negotiations may get, if you attract a qualified buyer, it is usually more advantageous to make concessions than to wait for another buyer. Escrows and closings can get bumpy, but keep focused on the outcome. You are eating up profits the longer you delay closing. However, if it becomes apparent that the buyer cannot or does not want to perform, then pull the plug sooner rather than later. Time is an expensive commodity.

My last piece of advice is, do not be tempted to spend the money from the proceeds of your sale until you have the cash in hand. It can be a painfully long way from "We love your house!" to "Here's your check."

Moonlighting

WILL SELL YOUR HOUSE FOR FOOD

Yes, times are tough.

Many of my colleagues are on sabbatical in Palm Springs. They have leased their houses in Los Angeles and live in condos in the desert, driving back for meetings and showings, their clients unaware of the zip code change.

Some of us have taken in family or renters to ease the financial stress. Some of us have additional part-time jobs like substitute teaching and designing jewelry. I do not have data, but I would imagine that many Realtors© all over the country have left the profession for jobs with dependable paychecks.

All of us are spending hours and hours working for nothing. Sellers change their minds or decide to lease instead of sell. Buyers can't find what they are looking for, banks decide not to loan at the last minute, properties don't appraise, bank executives take months to respond to offers on foreclosures, and on and on.

Many of us have lived through horrible sales conditions before. Like old soldiers telling war stories, we commiserate about when interest rates were 20 percent or when there was a writer's strike and the entertainment industry shut down.

Hopefully this recession and price correction cycle will soon be over, and we can begin to build equity again. Until then, if you are ready to sell, I wish you a swift and prosperous journey. Please be kind to your Realtor©. We are all having a tough time.

GLOSSARY

Buyers' Market: Market conditions in which there an abundance of properties for sale and a shortage of buyers. Thus, as in the rules of supply and demand, those in demand have the upper hand in negotiating.

Closing: Final sale, when the title or deed has been officially transferred to the buyer (or lender) in exchange for payment. In many states this occurs upon recordation of documents.

Coastal Commission: According to their website, they are a "quasi-judicial state agency" that "plans and regulates the land and water in the coastal plain" of California.

Comparables (comps): Properties that are similar or equivalent to the property being valued.

Comparative Market Analysis (CMA): A report outlining comparables that are currently on the market, are pending, and have recently sold. Information studied also includes the days on market for each property, variation between list price and sale price, average cost per square foot, market conditions, etc.

Counter offer: A new offer in response to an offer received. It contractually accepts the original offer subject to new terms and conditions that are itemized. If the counter offer is not accepted, the original offer is cancelled.

Curb Appeal: How charming and attractive a property is from the street.

Deferred maintenance: Deterioration of a property resulting from postponed maintenance.

Disclosure: Relevant information or material facts that affect a property or transaction.

Downward Market: An economical climate in which properties are continually losing value.

Escrow: The process in which money and documentation are held and overseen by a disinterested third party. This third party is also referred to as "Escrow".

Falling Market: The same as "downward market".

Foreclosure: A property that has been taken back by the lender as a result of non-payment from the borrower. These bank owned properties are often referred to as Real Estate Owned, or REO's.

Market Analysis: The same as "Comparable Market Analysis".

Market Value: The measure a property's worth by what an able buyer is willing to pay, and what a seller is willing to accept.

Multiple Listing Service: An area-wide marketing association composed of member brokers and agents who agree to share their listing information with each other.

Offer: A written document to a seller from a buyer outlining terms and conditions in which they agree to purchase a property.

Open House: A public open house is a specific window of time in which a property is open to the public for touring, traditionally Sunday afternoon. A brokers' open house is a time in which a property is open for agents to tour. Each area has a specific time during the week in which this occurs.

Over market: Above or greater than what the market will bear.

Sellers' Market: The opposite of Buyers' market. A condition in which there are many buyers compared to the amount of inventory, or homes listed for sale. Therefore, sellers have the advantage in negotiations.

Selling Season: The months of the year in which the greatest number of properties are traditionally sold. This varies region to region, but is usually in the late spring and summer due to school schedules and weather.

Short Sale: A situation in which the loan on a property is greater than the market value. In these cases the seller must get permission from the lender to sell the property at an amount less than what is owed.

Staging: The art of placing furniture and accessories in a property to make it more appealing to buyers.

Upside down: A seller is upside down on a property when the amount he owes the lender is greater than its market value.

www.ingramcontent.com/pod-product-compliance
Lightning Source LLC
Chambersburg PA
CBHW071256170526
45165CB00003B/1366